You & Me

Written By

Cheleesh Sai Sree

For my family & friends, thank you my beloved sister, Tejaswini A.S.C who inspired and introduced me to the world of writing.

A special thanks to Navyaka Kandula who is being introduced as an illustrator through this book. I would also like to thank Tejaswini Jakkoju, she is one of the reasons for the result of this book. Without these two individuals, may be these writings would have never been made into this book….

I don't know why suddenly, I feel all alone
I don't know why suddenly, I feel like crying
I don't know why suddenly, I become speechless

You become all alone because I'm not there beside you,
You start crying because you miss me,
You become speechless seeing me!

During these summer afternoons, the song in your voice, on that strings of the guitar is bringing peace within and a huge smile as if this is the absolutely right time to fall in love again with you.

Whenever I see you

Whenever you take a step forward towards me,

I take a step backward.

It's not because I don't love you.

It's because I may not remain forever beside you.

Your eyes speak about the truth,
Your smile speaks about your happiness,
Your face speaks about your emotion,
And me, I just want to see the truth, feel
your happiness and share your emotion.

Trusting a person is not an easy part,
But still, I want to trust you.
Believing what a person speak is impossible,
But I want to believe the words you speak.

What are the three difficult things for you?

–Saying a 'goodbye' to a close friend

–Saying a 'sorry' after a misunderstanding

–Saying an 'I love you' to the most beloved person.

“How come you’ve fallen for such a silent girl? ”, he asked.

Her silence speaks much more aloud than her words.

"Why are you getting irritated, seeing me?" , she asked.
"After you leave, I miss you.
And missing you is the most irritating thing to me" , he replied.

What is the worst thing that can happen to you?

Knowing that my ex-girlfriend & current girlfriend relation is like a relation between ketchup and fries.

Usually, people think I'm filled with only love, happiness, laughter, and excitement. But they don't know that I'm filled with hatred, sadness, anger, and depression.

Your smile is adorable, never let anyone steal it from you,

You act like a child, there is nothing wrong in it,

You are a bit short tempered, but still stay happy,

You are so pretty, that it can make anyone's heart start racing,

You are the one that no one can replace you.

When I met you for the first time,
I've felt me, in you.
You were a kind of an innocence that crept in the cool winter breeze.
Though you spread chills all over me,
it's worth feeling you.
You're just like a poem, but a poem seems incomplete without a rhythm which is me.
You're just like a way to meet its destination, where you are that destination.
You're not complete without me and I am not complete without you!!!

People do ask me, to explain about myself
in one line,
I would like to say, I'm just like a kind word
with stubborn heart.

If you want to know how much I love you,
then don't ask me to write
poems and stories..
You can find the countless love
in the twinkle of my eye when I smile,
looking at the person
in front of me which is you !!!...

"Sky looks more darker than usual.

Is it because I cannot see moon directly from my window?

It seems like the day had shifted to night pretty quick.

May be because I didn't give my eyes that chance to embrace the beauty beyond the monitor screen in front of me.

"I loved you with all the broken pieces of
my heart
not because I was expecting you to fix me.
But it is the only warmth which can slip
through gaps between those broken pieces
and can heal me."

I've always thought that you were cheating me with someone else, but I've never expected that you would be betraying me with that damn smile of yours by keeping every inch of pain within yourself.

Him: "Why did you lie to me? "
Her: "I didn't want you to be in pain"
Him: "What pain you have given is more compared to what we could face together"
Her: "I didn't want your feet to bleed by running on the thorns in my way, instead I just wanted to push you away from my road to a beautiful pavement filled with flowers. That is why I had to fake the direction of our lives."

What is your favorite place which brings peace to you?

- Any place which is surrounded with him brings peace within to me!

Youth is something which never comes
in life again & again, which makes one to
experience all the emotion.
It is as happy as a smile of an innocent.
As lovely as a rainy evening
As cold as a breezy winter night
As enthusiast as a sea wave which
touches the sad
As hard as a heart break
Youth is something unstoppable and worth
fighting for everything you need.

If I should write a about you in a single sentence, it would be like,

"You are one of the best chapters that I would pass through in the book of my life."

On one gloomy rainy afternoon,
you look like a morning summer sunshine.

Why do you trust her & adore her so much?

"Because when my wound is being cut
deeper and deeper, she has been a heal for,
that it made me to forget
the pain & scar of it."

If you want to know how much I love you,
then I suggest you peep through the poetry
I write, Each piece of the poem,
each word of the poem makes immense noise
shouting all the time describing how much I
love you with my whole heart.

Trust me,

"After every fall there is a bloom!"

In life there'll be many twisted tales,
but it is okay.

Some twists are worth, may be beautiful,
Different people, different choices,
different ways.
Some paths are worth crossing
and parting too!
Every meet with a person in your life
is worth a reason.

The sweetness of a chocolate is shared
among our dearest people to enjoy
any moment of celebration in life.
But you are a celebration which brings
sweetness in anyone's life.

Make how many plans you can, to break me down.

But remember, I will show you
the end of the master plan how it looks like,
in process of building myself up!

The moment I see myself smiling, makes me happy and makes me see through the beauty that exists in me.

Remember, your happiness is that smile of yours.

"Trust me, there will be a person who will always be glad to have your beautiful touch of memory in their lives."

Sometimes its better to leave some stories unsaid ···

Sometimes its better not to revise some chapters ···

Sometimes its better not to unfold some secrets ···

Sometimes its better not to revisit same city ···

Sometimes its better to leave some people at the same place where you left···

Though how many seasons come and go,
Still winters has its own essence to make
fall in love with them!

"You'd never believed in destiny till we met,
You'd stopped believing in destiny when
we fell apart!!
-In between fate happened!"

Remember you are that past in my life,
who brought happiness along with you
and a sting of pain leaving memories with
which I am left with now.

You are that song, which will be playing
always on my favorite list,

You are that music which I've always
danced for,
You are that rhythm, which I've always
hummed for,
You are that breeze, which I've enjoyed
all the time,
You are that star which made my life shine,
You are that hope which makes me live.

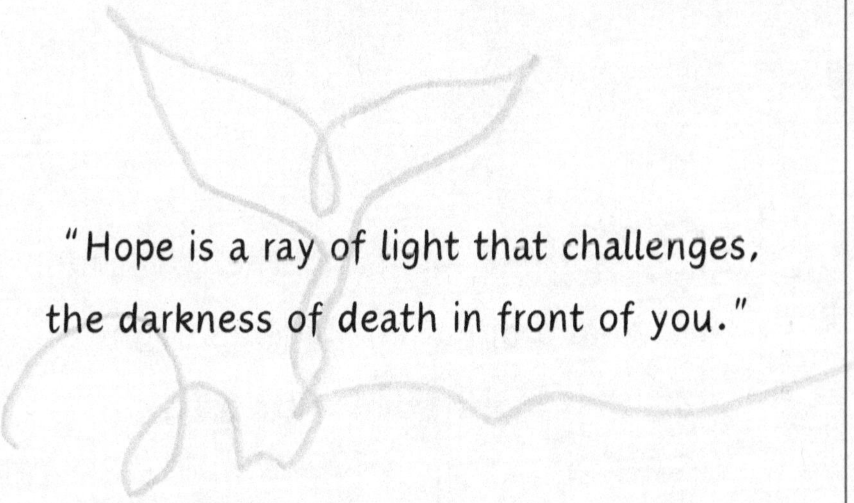

"Hope is a ray of light that challenges,
the darkness of death in front of you."

Every moment spent together; it made the world around me shine as bright as that night filled with stars.

"My every footstep behind you is not just
a journey to a destination,
Instead, it is the path where my heartbeat
followed."

What do you fear the most?

The silence I feel in a noisy crowd.

What does strength mean to you?

"Rising after every fall,

means strength to me."

Beautiful night, but it is long as if this
darkness is taking more time than usual
to end.
This beautiful night made me feel
more and more lonely without you.
It made my heart feel empty just like an
empty can though I should be feeling some
mixture of emotions.
Though I wanted to get a tight sleep,
I couldn't close my eyes because the
image of yours is never moving away from
my sight.
Night is beautiful but not anymore
when you aren't beside me.

In every corner of my mind, my urge to hug you one more time is getting strong and strong and strong every day. But yeah, I will wait until the situations are settling to make sure that we're falling all together again.

Let this world allow me to see all those colors
which I am surrounded with,
but every color makes me feel more vibrant
when I am with you.
That is how you make me feel!

I love to write letters to my near and dear,

While writing one for you,

it makes me fall for you more & deeper like a swirl.

Let a day be as exhausting as it could be
or may be more breaking,
At the same moment, a thought of your smile
always lifts up my spirits, my love!

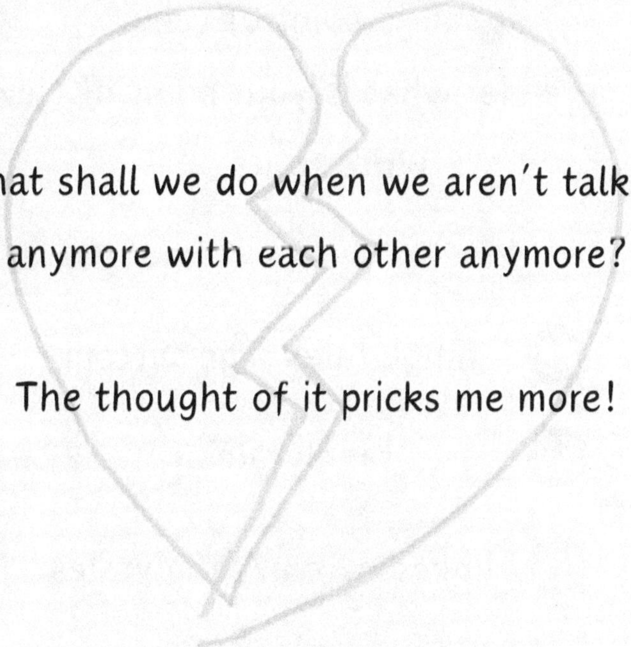

What shall we do when we aren't talking anymore with each other anymore?

The thought of it pricks me more!

All the illustrations in this book are author's point of view.

As a reader what is your point of view?

Write to us !

tanglytales@gmail.com

tanglytales

linkedin.com/tanglytales

tanglytales

www.ingramcontent.com/pod product compliance
Lightning Source LLC
LaVergne TN
LVHW041254150826
845673LV00008B/2589

* 9 7 9 8 8 9 1 8 6 7 2 4 6 *